KING COBRA

GARY SPROTT

Rourke
Educational Media

rourkeeducationalmedia.com

Fast Facts

Family: Elapidae

Genus: *Ophiophagus*

Number of species: 1

Species: *Ophiophagus hannah*

Diet: Snakes, lizards, rats, birds

Range: Bangladesh, Bhutan, Cambodia, China, Hong Kong, India, Indonesia, Laos, Malaysia, Myanmar, Nepal, Philippines, Singapore, Thailand, Vietnam

WORLD'S COOLEST SNAKES

Table of Contents

Fang-tastic Beast

The king cobra is one of the world's most amazing—and deadly—creatures. It's the longest venomous snake on the planet and can stretch as much as 18 feet (5.5 meters) from its flickering, forked tongue to the tip of its tail. That's about as long as a giraffe is tall!

Oh, and don't get a king cobra mad. This remarkable **reptile** can raise the front part of its body 6 feet (1.8 meters) off the ground, look you straight in the eye and growl like a mean dog! And, yes, its bite is worse than its bark.

Strange as it seems, the king cobra's deadly **venom** is used to keep humans healthy. Venom is collected from captured snakes to create a medicine known as antivenom to treat snakebite victims. The cobra's venom also is used to make painkillers.

A king cobra makes a meal of a rat snake.

Tassssty Treatsssss!

The king cobra feasts on rats, lizards, and birds. But it also has a taste for snake. That's what gives this cobra its scientific name, *Ophiophagus hannah*, which means "snake eater" in Greek.

Snakes are milked for venom at snake farms. Small amounts of venom may be injected into horses to produce antibodies that fight the snake's poison.

King cobras like to be close to water because
there is less change in temperature.

Like other reptiles, the king cobra gets its body heat from its surroundings. It lives in the wet, warm forests and swamps of Southeast Asia, including China, Thailand, the Philippines, and India.

The king cobra can spend a lot of time hanging out in bushes and trees, ready to drop in for a surprise visit. An unpleasant surprise!

Fact or Fiction?

King cobras are aggressive and go looking for trouble like a big bully.

FICTION! The cobra is shy and would rather slither away from danger. But be warned: the cobra will get nasty if it's cornered and when it's protecting its eggs.

Cold-Blooded Killer

The king cobra has evolved over thousands and thousands of years into a **magnificent** predator. It moves quickly over land and in water, hunting during the day and at night. It can spot a creature moving up to 330 feet (100 meters) away — that's about the length of a soccer field!

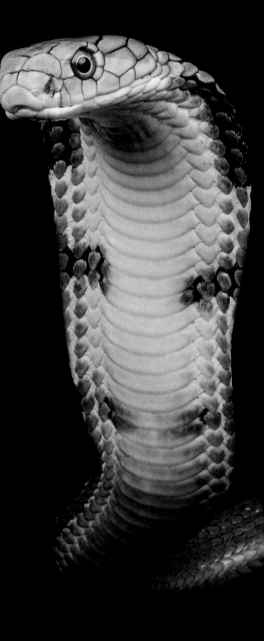

Fact or Fiction?

In their natural **habitat**, king cobras pose little threat to humans.

FACT! Researchers estimate only a handful of people are killed each year by king cobras, which usually live far from towns or villages.

The king cobra can strike over several feet in the blink of an eye. (Even though snakes can't blink because they don't have moveable eyelids!) When the king cobra bites, venom travels through its hollow fangs to **paralyze** its prey in minutes.

Cobra venom contains substances known as toxins that help the snake digest its prey.

Then it's time to dine. Like rubber bands, the king cobra's hinged jaws stretch open wide, wide, wide... and dinner is gulped down whole!

Mom won't want to hear this, but this snake doesn't chew its food. It only uses its teeth to move its meal down its tube-shaped body.

The king cobra's fangs are attached to its upper jaw and they're short—just 0.5 inches (12 millimeters)—so the snake doesn't bite itself by mistake. Have you ever bitten your tongue? Yup, it hurts. Now imagine how painful it would be if you had fangs instead of teeth!

inland taipan

Frightful Bite!

There are about 600 species of venomous snakes. The deadliest is the inland taipan of Australia, also known as the "Fierce Snake." The taipan is so **toxic**, one bite from this snake contains enough venom to kill 100 people.

A Royal Family

King cobras make their home in grasslands, mangrove marshes, and bamboo woods. Their scales may be black, green, or brown, with white or yellow highlights on the snake's back. This mix of colors helps the king cobra blend into its habitat, hiding it from prey and predators.

grasslands

bamboo woods

17

During breeding season, the female king cobra gives off a strong scent to attract a mate. Male cobras may compete for the female's attention by neck wrestling, with each snake trying to force its rival's head to the ground.

Scientists think some king cobras may breed with the same partner their whole lives.

After mating, the female will lay up to 40 eggs. The king cobra is the only species of snake that builds a nest for its eggs. The female uses her body like an arm to pile up leaves, soil, and branches to help keep her eggs warm.

The mother will **coil** herself on top of the nest to protect her eggs until they **hatch** in about 70 days. The male cobra usually hangs out nearby to help guard against attackers.

It can take up to four days for a king cobra to build a nest.

Slithering Noodles

There are about 3,400 species of snakes, from flying snakes to sea snakes. The smallest is the Barbados threadsnake. This little guy is only about four inches (10 centimeters) long—and as skinny as a spaghetti noodle!

Newborn cobras, or hatchlings, are about 15 to 20 inches (38 to 50 centimeters) long. The young snake is ready to hunt within days and its venom is just as dangerous as that of an adult cobra.

King cobras can live 20 years or more in the wild.

...e king cobra has earned its name

...ling over its kingdom. This **regal**

...nt has few natural enemies,

...y other king cobras, birds of prey

...as eagles, and the mongoose, a

...and razor-toothed mammal.

mongoose

eagle

I Look Good Enough to Eat!

The king cobra's diet includes other venomous snakes, even a hefty helping of king cobra! Yes, this snake is a cannibal.

Not only does the king cobra have tremendous eyesight, it can also flick out its long tongue to smell dinner—or danger. The snake then touches its tongue to special receptors in its mouth, known as the Jacobson's organ, to get a taste of its surroundings.

If it senses trouble, the king cobra will lift its upper body to scan the landscape and scare off predators.

And that's not all.

By stretching muscles and ribs, the snake can flatten its neck to create its famous hood—making it look even more fearsome!

hood ▶▶

Fact or Fiction?

The king cobra is also known as a *hamadryad*.

FACT! That name comes from ancient Greek mythology. It means "wood nymph."

Human destruction of forests and other habitats is major threat to the king cobra population, which has been declining for many years.

Industries such as logging and farming force king cobras out of

are the king cobra's
…nemy. In some
…he snake is hunted
…food, medicines,
…er goods. It is also
…lly as a pet.

cobra

Not Music to its Ears!

The snake charmers of India make money by pretending to **hypnotize** cobras with their flute music. But the snake doesn't hear the music. It reacts to the swaying of the flute.

Glossary

coil (KOIL): to wind something around and around into a series of loops

habitat (HAB-uh-tat): the place and natural conditions in which a plant or an animal lives

hatch (HACH): when a baby bird or reptile breaks out of an egg

hypnotize (HIP-nuh-tize): to put someone into a trance

magnificent (mag-NIF-i-sent): very impressive or beautiful

paralyze (PA-ruh-lize): to make someone or something helpless or unable to function

regal (REE-guhl): to do with or fit for a king or queen

reptile (REP-tile): a cold-blooded animal that crawls across the ground or creeps on short legs; reptiles have backbones and reproduce by laying eggs

toxic (TOK-sik): poisonous

venom (VEN-uhm): poison produced by some snakes and spiders; usually passed into a victim's body through a bite or sting

Index

Show What You Know

1. What are some of the animals eaten by the king cobra?
2. Why is a warm habitat like a swamp so important to a king cobra?
3. Why is venom collected from captured king cobras?
4. What are the king cobra's natural enemies?
5. How do people pose a threat to king cobras?

Further Reading

Hesper, Sam, *King Cobras*, PowerKids Press, 2015.

Gagne, Tammy, *Snakes: Built for the Hunt*, Capstone Press, 2016.

Hirsch, Rebecca E., *King Cobras: Hooded Venomous Reptiles*, Lerner, 2016.

About the Author

Gary Sprott is a writer in Tampa, Florida. He loves reading, watching soccer, and spending time at the beach with his family. He's not too scared of snakes—so long as they stay on the pages of a book!

Meet The Author!
www.meetREMauthors.com

www.rourkeeducationalmedia.com

PHOTO CREDITS: Cover: ©Matthijs Kuijpers/Alamy Stock Photo, p1: ©oariff, p4-5: ©bennymarty, p5: ©Juanmonino, p6, 16-17, 19: ©Malcolm Schuyl/Alamy Stock Photo, p6-7,: ©mark higgins/Alamy Stock Photo, p8: ©Vinod Goel / Alamy Stock Photo, p8-9: ©RSMultimedia/Alamy Stock Photo, p10: ©robas, p10-11: ©Sibons photography / Alamy Stock Photo, p12-13: ©Andreas Rose, p13: ©Luis Leamus/Alamy Stock Photo, p14: ©angelo giampiccolo / Alamy Stock Photo, p14-15: ©Norimages / Alamy Stock Photo, p17: ©tbradford, ©jimfeng, p18: ©Beetle2k42|Dreamstime.com, p19: ©Ian Thwaites / Alamy Stock Photo, p20-21: ©Avalon/Bruce Coleman Inc/Alamy Stock Photo, p22: ©blickwinkel/Alamy Stock Photo, p22-23: ©PHOTO.ZOOMMER.RU / Alamy Stock Photo, p24: ©dave stamboulis/Alamy Stock Photo, p24-25: ©Sean Cameron/Alamy Stock Photo, p26: ©Xavier Arnau, p27: ©pigphoto, p28: ©Valentin Shevchenko/Alamy Stock Photo, p28-29: ©DoubleO

Edited by: Keli Sipperley
Cover design by: Kathy Walsh
Interior design by: Rhea Magaro-Wallace

Library of Congress PCN Data

King Cobra / Gary Sprott

KING COBRA

GARY SPROTT

WORLD'S COOLEST SNAKES